Next Generation
ENERGY

# PUTTING EARTH FIRST

## Eating and Living Green

### Megan Kopp

CRABTREE
Publishing Company
www.crabtreebooks.com

# Crabtree Publishing Company

## www.crabtreebooks.com

**Author:** Megan Kopp

**Editors:** Sarah Eason and Jennifer Sanderson
and Petrice Custance

**Proofreader:** Katie Dicker

**Editorial director:** Kathy Middleton

**Design:** Paul Myerscough and Jessica Moon

**Cover design:** Paul Myerscough

**Photo research:** Sarah Eason and Jennifer Sanderson

**Prepress technician:** Tammy McGarr

**Print coordinator:** Margaret Amy Salter

Consultant: Richard Spilsbury, degree in Zoology,
author and editor of educational science books
for 30 years

Production coordinated by Calcium Creative

**Library and Archives Canada Cataloguing in Publication**

Kopp, Megan, author
    Putting Earth first : eating and living green / Megan Kopp.

(Next generation energy)
Includes index.
Issued in print and electronic formats.
ISBN 978-0-7787-2382-0 (bound).--
ISBN 978-0-7787-2386-8 (paperback).--
ISBN 978-1-4271-1759-5 (html)

    1. Sustainable living--Juvenile literature. 2. Environmental
protection--Citizen participation--Juvenile literature. I. Title.

GE195.5.K677 2016      j333.72      C2015-907829-6
                                    C2015-907830-X

**Library of Congress Cataloging-in-Publication Data**

Names: Kopp, Megan, author.
Title: Putting earth first : eating and living green / Megan Kopp.
Description: Crabtree Publishing Company, [2016] | Series:
   Next generation energy | Includes index. | Description based
   on print version record and CIP data provided by publisher;
   resource not viewed.
Identifiers: LCCN 2015045107 (print) | LCCN 2015044047 (ebook)
   | ISBN 9781427117595 (electronic HTML) | ISBN 9780778723820
   (reinforced library binding : alk. paper) | ISBN 9780778723868
   (pbk. : alk. paper)
Subjects: LCSH: Sustainable living--Juvenile literature. |
   Environmentalism--Juvenile literature.
Classification: LCC GE195.5 (print) | LCC GE195.5 .K674 2016
   (ebook) | DDC 640.28/6--dc23
LC record available at http://lccn.loc.gov/2015045107

# Crabtree Publishing Company

www.crabtreebooks.com     1-800-387-7650

Printed in Canada/012016/BF20151123

**Published in Canada**
**Crabtree Publishing**
616 Welland Ave.
St. Catharines, Ontario
L2M 5V6

**Published in the United States**
**Crabtree Publishing**
PMB 59051
350 Fifth Avenue, 59th Floor
New York, New York 10118

**Published in the United Kingdom**
**Crabtree Publishing**
Maritime House
Basin Road North, Hove
BN41 1WR

**Published in Australia**
**Crabtree Publishing**
3 Charles Street
Coburg North
VIC, 3058

# Contents

# Troubling Times

**Humans are using more resources than Earth has to offer. Resources are the sources of a country's wealth, such as minerals and land. Our increasing demand for resources has exceeded what our planet can provide. So what exactly does this mean?**

Humans are cutting down trees faster than they can be regrown. We harvest more fish than oceans can replenish, or replace. We send more **carbon dioxide** into the **atmosphere** by burning **fossil fuels** than forests and oceans can absorb, or take in. In fact, it would take approximately one-and-a-half Earths just to keep up with the rate at which we are currently using resources.

The amount of land and natural resources needed to produce the goods and services we use to support our lifestyles is called our **ecological footprint**. This measure can be for an individual, a region, or the entire world population. Not everyone is using the world's resources equally. Some are using more than others.

Average ecological footprints are larger in some areas than others. This graph shows how many planets would be needed if everyone on Earth had the same footprint as the average residents of the countries listed below.

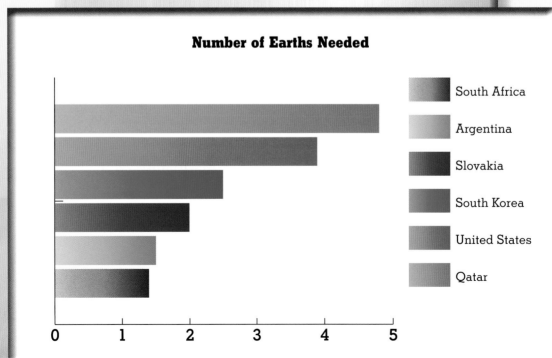

**Number of Earths Needed**

- South Africa
- Argentina
- Slovakia
- South Korea
- United States
- Qatar

0 1 2 3 4 5

## Supporting Life As We Know It

Human activities have the ability to drive change on a global scale. With the current pace of **climate change**, there is a real possibility that we will irreversibly change life on Earth. The quality of life on Earth depends on our actions. The key is sustainability, or the ability to conserve resources and use them efficiently. Everything we need for our survival and well-being depends, either directly or indirectly, on the natural environment. We cannot keep using more resources than the planet can supply in the long term.

Three billion people rely on fish and other seafood for protein. We used to think the supply was endless. We now know this is simply not true.

## FAST FORWARD

Scientists have calculated the amount of Earth's resources the global population can use each year based on the amount of resources Earth is able to renew each year. Every year, since the 1960s, we have used more resources than the planet can replace. Earth **Overshoot** Day marks the precise day each year when this overuse of resources begins. In 1970, that day was December 23, in 2000 it was October 4, and in 2015, it was August 13. We keep "borrowing" from the next year's resources, but eventually there will be nothing left to borrow. What date do you think Earth Overshoot Day will be in 2030? Does that date concern you? Give reasons for your answer.

# The Green-Living Movement

In 1954, a book called *Living the Good Life* raised attention to the topic of sustainable living. The authors, Helen and Scott Nearing, promoted self-sufficiency based on their experiences. Eight years later, Rachel Carson wrote *Silent Spring.* Carson's book brought awareness to the hazardous use of human-made **pesticides** and their effect on the health of Earth's fragile **ecosystems**. In the 1960s, activists began promoting green living, and drew attention to environmental issues around the world.

It took another 30 years, but the 1992 United Nations' Earth Summit in Rio de Janeiro, Brazil, brought together governments and organizations to discuss environmental issues. They talked about using alternative sources of energy to replace the use of fossil fuels, and the need for expanding public transportation systems to decrease vehicle **emissions**. In 2007, the United Nations published a document promoting sustainable lifestyles in communities and homes.

The recycling symbol, called the Mobius Loop, represents the cycle of using and re-using materials in a sustainable way.

## Living Green

Living green refers to living in a sustainable way. To live green, we need to reduce our energy needs and eat **organic** and locally produced food. Living green begins with understanding that the choices we make affect everyone. Our choices have an effect today and in the future. We need to conserve our natural resources and preserve our environments because they provide us with air, water, food, shelter, and energy where we live, learn, work, and play.

Reducing our energy use and using fewer harmful chemicals are ways to live green. Simple actions, such as walking instead of driving to the grocery store, and buying locally grown vegetables instead of produce shipped over long distances, are other examples.

To reduce their environmental impact, many people ride bikes or walk to their destinations instead of using vehicles that burn fossil fuels.

# REWIND

Before modern times, people lived off the land, raising crops and animals. Today, the majority of the world's population lives in cities. Do you think we would be concerned about green living if we still lived a more rural lifestyle? Support your answer with examples from this book.

# Why Is Green Good?

**We use energy to light and heat our homes, power our electronics, and transport ourselves to school and work. It takes energy to produce, transport, store, and prepare foods.**

Energy use is a key factor contributing to climate change. One of the major causes of climate change is a buildup of **greenhouse gases**, such as carbon dioxide and **methane**. These greenhouse gases are trapping heat from the Sun in the atmosphere, which warms up our planet. This is called global warming. Climate change is happening so fast that many species of plants and animals cannot adapt quickly enough to cope with the change. Ice caps are melting, which makes sea levels rise. Carbon dioxide and other **pollutants** left over from human activity are the biggest factors in the growth of our ecological footprint.

## Go Green, Go!

One way to reduce our ecological footprint is to cut down on our use of nonrenewable forms of energy. These are natural resources that took millions of years to be created deep in Earth. We have a limited supply and cannot make more. Earth is running out of many of these natural resources.

The habitats of birds and many other species of wildlife are affected by climate change.

Nonrenewable resources include fossil fuels, such as oil, natural gas, and coal, as well as **radioactive** materials, such as uranium, which are used to generate nuclear power. Approximately three-quarters of all carbon dioxide emissions come from burning fossil fuels to generate electricity. Switching to renewable forms of energy is another way we can reduce our ecological footprint. Renewable energy is energy from a source that will never run out. It includes solar energy from the Sun, wind energy, geothermal energy from heat inside Earth, **biomass** from organic plant and animal matter, and hydropower from flowing water.

When we choose to reduce our energy consumption and switch to renewable resources for energy production, we can make a positive impact on climate change.

Greenhouse gases may not be visible to our eyes, but they have a major impact for all life on Earth.

## The Energy Future: You Choose

By 2050, Earth's population is predicted to grow by two billion people. Supplying food, water, and energy will continue to be major issues. Climate change and the **depletion** of ecosystems and natural resources will make this even more challenging. What do you think our world will look like in 2050 if we do not make any changes to how we use Earth's resources? Explain your answer.

# Energy Choices

In 2012, 13.2 percent of the world's energy supply was from renewable sources. Just one year later, this had increased to 22 percent. Using renewable resources will help limit global warming. Even though these are very positive effects, nonrenewable resources continue to power most of the world's energy use.

The reasons for the slow change to renewable energy are complex. One of the major factors is cost. The production of wind, solar, tidal, and hydro power is expensive. Subsidies, or financial incentives from governments, can help encourage the development of improved technology, performance, and delivery of sustainable power. Eventually, the price of renewable energy will come down. However, changes such as this must start at a governmental level. As citizens, we can do our part by **investing** in green energy choices ourselves. We can influence our government representatives to push for green technology subsidies. If enough people demand change, it will happen.

Carbon dioxide and methane are greenhouse gases. Levels of greenhouse gases are higher today than they have ever been in the past 650,000 years.

# A Question of Carbon

A **carbon footprint** is a measure of the amount of carbon dioxide released when a person or group uses fossil fuels. Since we still rely on fossil fuels for most of our energy needs, our carbon footprint continues to grow. As our population expands, more land is needed for building, so forests are cut down. This adds to global warming because forests are **carbon sinks**. Trees absorb carbon emissions, so when forests are destroyed, there is nothing to prevent carbon dioxide from accumulating in the atmosphere.

The Intergovernmental Panel on Climate Change recommends phasing out the use of fossil fuels by 2070. This is not impossible. Denmark, for example, has reduced its carbon emissions by 33 percent since the 1990s.

Transportation—whether by sea, sky, or road—is a major contributor to carbon dioxide emissions.

## The Energy Future: You Choose

In 2013, there was a shift to try to create more new energy from renewable energy sources than from fossil fuel energy sources. In Norway, 98 percent of electricity produced comes from renewable energy sources. Only 13.7 percent of the United States' electricity production comes from renewable sources. In 2011, only 1.3 percent of Canadian homes used renewable energy sources. Do you think countries such as the United States and Canada need to expand their capacity for renewable energy sources? Support your answers with examples from this book.

# Energy to Burn

**The United States economy is heavily dependent on industry, which uses a lot of energy. Industry is responsible for 31.9 percent of the nation's overall energy consumption. Most of this goes toward the refining, or purifying, of petroleum and the manufacturing of steel, aluminum, paper, chemicals, and cement. Petroleum refining and the chemical industry are the biggest energy users of all industries.**

The good news is that industries are working to reduce their energy consumption. Today's petroleum refineries use about 30 percent less energy than they did 40 years ago. Over the past 25 years, the steel industry has managed to reduce its energy consumption by 30 percent for every ton of steel. It now takes 20 percent less energy to produce 1 pound (0.45 kg) of aluminum than it did 20 years ago. New technology has increased energy efficiency in the chemical industry by more than 50 percent in the last 35 years. The pulp and paper industry today uses 30 percent less fossil fuels than it did in the past. Cement plants have reduced their energy consumption by more than 30 percent.

There may be plenty of fossil fuels in the ground, but the Earth has a limited capacity for how much it can withstand humans burning these fuels.

## Recycling Is Key

Recycling refers to making something new from something that has been used before. Using recycled materials to make a product helps save energy. For example, it requires 75 percent less energy to recycle steel than to make it brand new from iron ore. Today, two-thirds of new steel is made from recycled scrap. This makes steel the leading recycled product in the United States. Similarly, using recycled aluminum requires 95 percent less energy than making it from mined resources.

Recycling reduces the amount of paper in **landfills**, which means cutting down fewer trees. Recycling also provides an opportunity to use energy that normally would be ignored in landfills. For example, waste products such as printing inks, dry cleaning fluids, and old tires can be used as fuel. Many cement plants in the United States use waste as fuel, meeting between 20 and 70 percent of their energy needs. These waste items have a high energy content. For example, 1 pound (0.45 kg) of tires has more energy than 1 pound (0.45 kg) of coal.

Our environment depends on industries reducing their energy consumption.

## REWIND

In the late 1700s, life changed around the world. The invention of machine power led to an **industrial revolution**. Industry began to move from farms to factories, and cities grew. Life became easier for some as factories were able to mass produce everything from clothing to cars. There was a price to pay, however. As more people became reliant on mass production, more and more energy was required. The production process used natural resources and polluted the environment. Although society will never return to a pre-industrial- revolution lifestyle, living green can help reduce its impact.

# Living Green

**Manufacturing the goods we use every day takes a huge amount of energy. The industrial sector of the United States' economy consumes almost one-third of the total energy used in the country. As consumers, we can reduce industrial energy use through our product choices, and how we dispose of packaging or products we no longer use.**

## Waste Not, Want Not

For example, Canadians contribute almost 6.4 pounds (2.9 kg) of garbage per person to landfills every day. The most effective way for consumers to help reduce the amount of energy consumed by industry is to decrease the number of unnecessary products produced, and to reuse or repair items whenever possible.

Buy only what you need. Purchasing fewer goods means that there is less to throw away. It also means that fewer goods will need to be produced, so less energy will be used in the manufacturing process. Buying goods with less packaging also reduces the amount of waste generated and the amount of energy used.

It is estimated that more than 100,000 marine animals are killed each year due to plastic debris in the ocean.

Buy products that can be used repeatedly. If you buy things that can be reused rather than **disposable** items, which are used once and thrown away, you will save natural resources. You will also save the energy used to make disposable products and reduce the amount of landfill space needed to contain their waste.

Many people throw broken products away and buy new ones. Many of these products could be easily and cheaply repaired. Consider repairing a product before throwing it away. This saves energy, money, and natural resources.

Using recycled material almost always consumes less energy than using new materials. Recycling reduces energy needs for mining, refining, and many other manufacturing processes.

The average person tosses more than 67 pounds (30 kg) of used clothing into the landfill every year.

# FAST FORWARD

The Great Pacific Garbage Patch is an island of plastic waste in the Pacific Ocean. It is twice as large as the continental United States. Plastic does not biodegrade, or break down completely. It breaks down only into smaller pieces. Scientists have collected up to 1.9 million pieces of plastic in 1 square mile (750,000 pieces per sq km) of the Great Pacific Garbage Patch. It grows in size each year. What should we do about it? Explain your answer.

# The Four Rs

**Reduce, reuse, repair, and recycle—these "Four Rs" are the main principles of living green. Look around your home and see what you can do to reduce, reuse, repair, and recycle to help your family use less energy in your daily lives.**

Reducing refers to using fewer resources. It is the most effective way to make a difference. To start with, reduce the power that you use by unplugging devices when you are not using them. Replace regular **incandescent** light bulbs with compact fluorescent bulbs, which use about 75 percent less energy. When you shop, avoid unnecessary packaging. Look for items that will last because purchases can have a long-term impact.

Before people used paper towels and napkins, they used reuseable cloth products. Instead of using paper towels, take old towels and cut them into rags for messy spills. Reuse glass jars to organize and safely store things. Buy reusable drink bottles and reusable cutlery for your lunchbox instead of packing disposable spoons and forks.

## A Disposable Society

We have become a disposable society, which means that we often buy new goods rather than repair the old. For example, if the heel is damaged on a pair of shoes, we buy a new pair. In our society, it is easier to shop than to repair something broken.

Before it closed, Puente Hills was the largest U.S. landfill. Trash was piled as high as a 40-story building and covered an area close in size to New York City's Central Park.

Sometimes, it is cheaper to buy a new product than to repair an old one. Electronics can be more expensive to repair than to replace. Replacing is easier on the bank account, but repairing is easier on the environment.

Recycling is the last step of the four Rs. If you cannot reduce, reuse, or repair, then it is time to recycle. All products, including paper, plastic, and aluminum, can be recycled. Recycling reduces energy needs for mining, refining, and many other manufacturing processes. Recycling saves cents and makes sense.

Close to 900,000 tons (816,466.3 metric tons) of plastic bottles were recycled in the United States in 2013.

## The Energy Future: You Choose

We have the ability to turn trash into treasure, but we seem to do it only as a last resort. The Landfill Harmonic is an orchestra in which teenagers play instruments made from materials found in landfills. The music they create is magical. The Landfill Harmonic began because the musicians could not afford to buy new instruments. What do you think it will take to change the idea that new products are always better than used? Give reasons for your answers.

# Eating Green

**Food and energy are tied together. Food production uses 30 percent of the world's energy. It takes energy to plant, harvest, store, and deliver food products. Eating green does not reduce the need for planting and harvesting. When we grow our own food or buy locally produced food, however, we drastically reduce the amount of energy used in transportation and storage.**

Eating locally produced food reduces the carbon dioxide emissions related to the transporting, processing, and refrigerating of foods imported from far away. Many of the fruits and vegetables we find in supermarkets travel over 1,500 miles (2,414 km) before reaching our homes. An average meal travels about 932 miles (1,500 km) from a farm to our plates.

The production of meat is a major contributor to climate change. Raising livestock for food is not an efficient use of energy and water. Large amounts of both resources are required for the production, processing, and transporting of meat.

Eating green also includes making organic choices. Organic food choices help limit the production of pesticides and fertilizers, which are often made from fossil fuels. The manufacturing and transportation of these chemicals uses large amounts of energy. If you eat organic, you help avoid using these chemicals. Organic foods also taste good, and have more vitamins and minerals.

## Food Waste

Eating green also means avoiding waste whenever possible. Almost one-third of all food produced worldwide is wasted. Food is thrown away during processing and transporting, in supermarkets, and at home in our kitchens. We have little control outside our homes, but we can control how the amount of food we waste in our kitchens. According to an American organization called the Natural Resources Defense Council, two-thirds of food wasted is the result of food spoiling before being eaten. The remaining third is from cooking or serving too much.

Growing your own food is good for the environment.

## FAST FORWARD

Canadians use around 55 million plastic bags a week. In March of 2007, Leaf Rapids, Manitoba, became the first Canadian town to ban single-use plastic bags. This is an important step toward sustainable packaging. However, the plastic industry claims plastic bags are more environmentally friendly than reusable bags because they take up less landfill space when their use is over. They also take less resources to produce. Based on this, do you think other cities will ban plastic bags in the future? Give reasons for your answer.

# Compost and Grow

**Approximately 220 million tons (199.58 million metric tons) of waste is sent to landfills in the United States every year. Landfills are the third-largest source of human-related methane emissions. Methane traps more heat in the atmosphere than carbon dioxide.**

Two-thirds of household waste does not need to go to landfills. Organic materials such as yard trimmings, food scraps, wood waste, paper, and paperboard products are the largest contributor to our trash. Instead, they can be **composted**. Composting improves the quality of soil. Using food waste in compost, such as vegetable peelings and egg shells, feeds the soil and retains nutrients naturally.

In 2011, the 27 states in the European Union composted, on average, 15 percent of city waste. Austria composted the most, with 34 percent, while France, Spain, and Germany each composted about 18 percent. In 1990, only 2 percent of all of the solid waste created in the United States was composted. Today, 20 percent of total solid waste is composted in the United States. This includes over 60 percent of all yard waste.

Using compost on a vegetable garden helps reduce the amount of energy, fuel, water, and pollution associated with large-scale industrial **agriculture**.

## Ways to Compost

Today, there are hundreds of composting programs in smaller communities across North America. Larger cities such as San Francisco, Seattle, San Antonio, Toronto, and Portland (OR) are jumping on board. New York City is even piloting a composting program.

If composting your waste is not an option, **vermiposting** may be a solution. In vermiposting, worms eat their way through the waste. It is popular in apartments without backyards. If you cannot compost and the thought of red wiggler worms makes you queasy, check around your neighborhood to see if there is a community garden that will accept your organic household waste for compost.

### FAST FORWARD

In 1960, the average person produced about 2.7 pounds (1.2 kg) of waste a day. Today, that number is 4.3 pounds (1.9 kg). Do you think that composting will keep that number from increasing in the future? Give reasons for your answer.

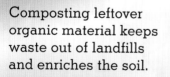

Composting leftover organic material keeps waste out of landfills and enriches the soil.

# Shrinking Your Footprint

Everything we use seems to be made on a larger scale now. In 1973, the average size of a home in the United States was 1,600 square feet (148.64 sq m). In 2013, this increased to 2,679 square feet (248.89 sq m). Cars and trucks of the same make and model have grown in size since the 1970s. We cannot necessarily control these factors, but we can make changes in our personal habits to reduce energy waste.

Reduce your energy consumption by increasing your home's energy efficiency. Talk to your parents or caregivers about getting energy-efficient appliances. Investigate green-power options and research purchasing electricity generated from renewable energy sources, such as Canada's Bullfrog Power. Bullfrog Power puts clean, renewable energy on the grid and green natural gas into pipelines. Since 2005, the company has funded more than 60 green-energy projects.

List the things you can do to shrink your footprint, and then share your list with your family.

You can choose to travel sustainably. Travel by bicycle, carpool with friends, or take the city bus. To use less water, take showers instead of baths. It takes energy to lift water from aquifers, pump it through canals and pipes, and control its flow.

## Eco-Friendly Choices

Learn how to make eco-friendly consumer purchases. Skip the pretty packages and buy in bulk. Most packaging is made from polyethylene. This plastic is made from oil and natural gas, which are both nonrenewable resources.

You can do research to choose your computer carefully. Although laptops are more energy efficient, desktop computers last longer. Whichever device you use, be sure to power down when not in use. That means turning it off at the outlet, not just the device, because supply continues to draw power, even when the electronics are turned off.

Skip the individual bags for your vegetables and the plastic bag for your groceries. Use a paper or reusable bag instead.

# REWIND

Paper grocery bags were invented in 1852. By 1870, paper bags were found in almost every retail store. Before that time, canvas bags, wooden boxes, and crates were used to carry purchases home. By the late 1970s, disposable plastic bags were found everywhere. By 2000, more than 4 billion bags were being discarded each year. Today, if the discarded bags were placed side by side, there would be enough to circle the globe 63 times. Do you think plastic bags are a useful aid or an unnecessary pollutant? Explain your answer.

# It's Not Always Easy Being Green

**As consumers, we have a responsibility to look for products from companies that are committed to using recycled goods in their manufacturing. For example, we can choose to purchase books and magazines from a printer that uses recycled paper.**

Sometimes, identifying if a product is sustainable can be confusing. Competitors do not always agree on what makes a product sustainable. They have different ways of labeling and marketing their "environmentally friendly" products. Most people understand the generic symbol used to show recycled content. However, the symbol can also sometimes be used to indicate that the product can be recycled. It does not mean that the product meets all "green" standards. Similarly, if a product is advertised as "organic," this may not necessarily be true.

We need stores to come to an agreement on meaningful and easy-to-understand product information. It would be good if there were standard labels for packaging, shelves labeled by retailers, and a separate green purchase aisle in stores. Governments, businesses, and consumers need to start working together to achieve goals like these.

PLASTIC PAPER CANS

By Law

Color-coded recycling bins make it easy to recycle properly. If only it was this easy to figure out green purchasing!

## Getting Together

When competitors work together and there is a consistent message, it is easily understood. The Ecolabel Index is a global directory that explains almost 450 labels related to products and companies. These are some of its labels:

- Energy Star—identifies energy efficient electrical products.

- Forest Stewardship Council (FSC) Certified—assures products (mainly paper and wood) have been produced sustainably. This means the production of these products did not destroy forests and supported the biodiversity of wildlife.

- Fair Trade—the products with this label meet social, economic, and environmental standards. This label is often used in the coffee and chocolate industries, because these products often come from areas in poverty. Fair Trade ensures that these people are paid fairly for their goods.

Picking up trash is a reaction to a problem that has already occurred. Reducing the amount of disposable items is a **proactive** solution before a problem occurs.

## The Energy Future: You Choose

The Story of Stuff project began in 2007 with the release of a movie about the way we make, use, and throw away all the "stuff" in our lives. The original movie was followed by two more: *The Story of Change* and *The Story of Solutions*. You can watch these videos at http://storyofstuff.org. Do you think that sustainable changes need to be made to what we manufacture and how we do it? Why or why not?

# Step into Action

**Many children and teenagers think that green living choices need to come from adults. This is not true. Each and every person can make decisions that can help reduce energy usage.**

American Gabrielle Posard was 12 years old when she took action on hunger and food waste in 2009. She began encouraging grocers to donate their surplus or short-dated food. To date, Gabrielle's team at Donate Don't Dump has saved more than 1 million pounds (453,593 kg) of food from going into landfills. Gabrielle's mission is to make food rescue as common as recycling. In 2013, she won the U.S. President's Environmental Youth Award.

Another winner of the same award is Pavan Gowda. When he was eight, Pavan started a nonprofit organization called Green Kids Now, Inc. He believes we should care for the planet by conserving energy and water, adopting alternative resources, and striving for a **zero waste** community. Pavan's ideas led to the creation of the Green Kids Conference. The Green Kids Conference allows interested children and their families to learn more about sustainable living.

On his twelfth birthday, Danny Seo founded Earth 2000. He has been campaigning for sustainability ever since. Now in his late 30s, Danny runs a widely read magazine and a line of eco-friendly home and food products. He is also the best-selling author of nine books, including the *Upcycling* series, which features eco-friendly craft projects.

Actions often speak louder than words. Planting trees can make a big difference.

## Green Goals

At 14, Mayelly Guzman in Lima, Peru, was motivated to learn about recycling for an eco-business after seeing the adults in her community ignore the garbage piling up around them. Since then, she has been busy teaching younger children how to make products with recycled materials. She spreads her message at fairs, universities, and businesses in her community. Mayelly's video *Reto Verde*, or *Green Goal*, won the 2015 Adobe Youth Voices award for Social Venture.

If we do not stand up and start fighting for our planet, who will?

## FAST FORWARD

In 2005, 13-year-old Erin Schrode and her mother launched a green campaign for cosmetics. It is found at www.teensturninggreen.org. They created a list of dangerous ingredients, products that contain them, and safe, sustainable alternatives. They lobby for laws banning substances in cosmetics such as lead in lipstick. How much impact do you think this kind of activism has on cosmetic companies as they plan product development? Give reasons for your answer.

# Power Up!

You have read about the problems our planet faces and seen some easy things you can do to help. Living and eating green means practicing sustainability, reducing energy needs, and eating organic and local.

## What Can You Do?

Eating and living green involves awareness and action on both a global and a local level. Simple actions such as replacing light bulbs, turning off computers, and cycling to school can have a large impact if we all do it. It is important to know where our foods come from and to buy local foods in a sustainable way. Growing fruit and vegetables in our own gardens is no longer a thing of the past, but the way of the future. Choosing renewable resources for our energy production is a sustainable path to follow.

Eating and living green is the right choice for our planet.

# Activity:

The Sun is the most important renewable energy source. To harness its power, energy must be converted from visible light into heat or electricity. This simple solar oven shows you how this can be done.

## You Will Need:

- Black spray paint
- Shoebox
- Tape measure
- Pencil
- Large sheets of cardboard
- Pair of scissors
- Aluminum foil
- Adhesive spray
- Duct tape
- Shredded newspaper
- Aluminum baking tin
- Sliced carrots
- 1 large oven bag
- Oven mitts
- Help from an adult

## Instructions

1. Spray paint the inside of the shoebox.
2. Cut two trapezoidal cardboard pieces with a top width of 20 inches (51 cm), bottom width of 6 inches (15 cm), and height of 23.5 inches (60 cm).
3. Cut another two cardboard pieces with a top width of 25.5 inches (65 cm), bottom width of 12 inches (30 cm), and center height of 23.5 inches (60 cm).
4. Cover one side of each cardboard piece with foil.
5. Put cardboard pieces foil side down. Place them side-by-side, narrow to wide end, to form a semi-circle.
6. Tape the panels together along their seams.
7. Flip over the panels. Tape their inner seams.
8. Stand the panels upright, foil side in, and tape the final seam to make a reflector cone.
9. Tape the shoebox to the bottom of the reflector. Attach a cardboard stand to the oven to support it.
10. Take the oven outside in the sunshine.
11. Add the carrots to the baking tin, cover with the oven bag, and put inside the shoebox. Leave to cook.

**reflector**

**shoebox**

**stand**

## What Happened?

Dark surfaces absorb light and become warm. The oven gathered sunlight from a wide area using reflective surfaces, making it hot enough to cook the vegetables.

# Glossary

**Please note: Some bold-faced words are defined where they appear in the text**

**agriculture** The science or practice of farming

**atmosphere** The layer of gases that surround Earth

**biomass** Organic material such as plants or animal waste

**carbon dioxide** A gas molecule made of a carbon atom joined with two oxygen atoms

**carbon footprint** The amount of carbon dioxide that is released as a result of the use of fossil fuels by a particular person or group

**carbon sinks** Natural or artificial reservoirs that gather and store some carbon-containing chemical compounds. Carbon sinks remove carbon dioxide from the atmosphere

**climate change** Changes to the usual weather patterns in an area or the entire Earth

**composted** Using food waste, such as vegetable peelings and egg shells, to improve the quality of soil

**depletion** A reduction in the number of something

**disposable** Used once and then thrown away

**ecological footprint** A method for calculating how much land or water a group of humans needs, to produce all the resources it uses to live

**ecosystems** The plants, animals, and other organisms that live together in specific environments

**emissions** The production and discharge of something, especially gas

**fossil fuels** Energy sources made from the remains of plants and animals that died millions of years ago and were buried

**greenhouse gases** Gases like carbon dioxide and methane that contribute to the greenhouse effect

**incandescent** Emitting light as a result of being heated

**industrial revolution** A rapid change where countries become more focused on using machines to make goods

**industry** The making or producing of goods or services

**investing** Using money to make a profit or more money

**landfills** Places to dispose of garbage and other waste material by burying it

**manufacturing** Making something on a large scale using machinery

**methane** A colorless, odorless gas

**organic** Produced without adding artificial chemicals. It can also be a material that was formerly living and contains carbon

**overshoot** To go past a point unintentionally as a result of not being able to stop

**pesticides** Substances used to kill insects that are harmful to plants

**petroleum** Crude oil

**pollutants** Substances introduced into the environment that cause harmful or poisonous effects

**proactive** Acting in anticipation of future problems, needs, or changes

**radioactive** Giving off high-energy rays and particles

**vermiposting** Using worms to break down organic material

**zero waste** No garbage being sent to landfills

# *Learning More*

Find out more about living sustainably.

## Books

Baker, Imogen. *Recycle, Reuse, Renew! 70 Outstanding DIY Projects and DIY Household Hacks for Your Home.* Amazon Digital Services, Inc., 2015.

Elliot, Marion. *Recycled Craft Projects for Kids: 50 Fantastic Things to Make from Junk.* Armadillo Books, 2014.

Gay, Kathlyn. *Living Green: The Ultimate Teen Guide* (It Happened to Me). Scarecrow Press, 2012.

Pollan, Michael. *The Omnivore's Dilemma: Young Reader's Edition.* Dial Books, 2015.

## Websites

Find out more about the David Suzuki Foundation and living green at:
**www.davidsuzuki.org/what-you-can-do**

Learn about the Natural Resources Defense Council: The Green Squad at:
**www.nrdc.org/greensquad/intro/intro_1.asp**

Recognize the ecosymbols of the Ecolabel Index at:
**www.ecolabelindex.com/ecolabels**

Watch videos on the National Science Foundation website at:
**www.nsf.gov/news/special_reports/greenrevolution/index.jsp**

# Index